Writings of a Poet
"Written from the Heart"

"He lifted me out of the slimy pit, out of the mud and the mire. He set my feet on a rock and gave me a firm place to stand. He put a new song in my mouth, a hymn of praise to our God. Many will see and fear and put their trust in the Lord." Psalm 40:2-3

Bryan Lewis

UWriteit Publishing Company
www.uwriteitpublishingcompany.com
Goldsboro, NC USA

Writings of a Poet by Bryan Lewis
Copyright © 2012 by Bryan Lewis
www.writingsofapoet.com

ALL RIGHTS RESERVED

ISBN: ISBN- 13: 978-0615605777

ISBN- 10: 061560577X

First Printing March – 2012

NO PART OF THIS BOOK MAY BE REPRODUCED IN ANY FORM, BY PHOTOCOPYING OR BY ANY ELECTRONIC OR MECHANICAL MEANS, INCLUDING INFORMATION STORAGE OR RETRIEVAL SYSTEMS, WITHOUT PERMISSION IN WRITING FROM THE COPYRIGHT OWNER/AUTHOR

Unless otherwise indicated, scripture quotations in this book are from the King James Version.

This publication is designed to provide information regarding the subject matter covered. It is published with the understanding that the author is not engaged in rendering legal counsel or other professional services. If legal advice or other professional advice is required, the services of a professional person should be sought.

Printed in the U.S.A.

Dedication

This book is dedicated to my Lord and Savior Jesus Christ. Without him I would not be here. Also, my loving parents Billy and Patricia Lewis. Father you have shown me how to be a gentleman and a real man of God. You have always been in my corner and you have shown me what hard work and perseverance will do for a man. Mother you have shown me what it is to be strong and love hard. You are a constant supporter and I love you from the bottom of my heart. To my biological parents wherever you are; thank you for giving me a chance to live. Thank you for giving your son a chance to have a better life. I can't wait for the day I get to meet you. I love you and there's always a place for y'all in my heart. Last but not least to a very special woman in my life Jasmine Brewington. We have grown up together and created a bond that's unbreakable. You have supported me through a lot and I thank God for you. You inspired some of these poems and as a friend I appreciate your love throughout these years. Peace and blessings to everyone. Love, live, life.

Table of Contents

Writings Of My Heart
Aunt Brenda	7
Grandma	9
Feeling	10
I See Her	12
It's Time Now	14
Something About You	16
Still Someone Special	18
What This Is	20
What Was Done	22

Writings Of My Pain, Passion
Abuse, Pain, You	24
His Mistake	26
Hurt	28
Addicted to My Spouse	30

Writings Of My Love
Because Of You	32
Final Destination	34
I'm Here	36
How I Feel	38
My Ode to You	41
Our Love	44
Promises	46
The Proposal	48
What I See In You	51
Why I Love You, Its Many Meanings	55
Your Love	57

The Love Trilogy
Love Part 1	60
Love Is…Love Part 2	62
Love…The Final Part	66

Writings Of My Life, Life Lessons
A Good Man	72
All I Want In A Woman	76
Angels Cry	80
How to Treat A Lady	82
I Never Asked	86
Life Lessons in Wisdom	91
Unthinkable…I'm Ready	96
What I Can Do For A Woman	98
The Black Woman	101

A Love Letter To Poetry
My Ode to Poetry	104
More Than Poetry, More Than Words	107
Poems Don't Have to Rhyme, We Will Get Through This	111
Why I Write Poetry	114

Introduction

This is my very first book of any kind. I've been writing poetry since I was 6 years old. I never knew that I would develop so much passion for it through the years. I'm blessed to say these are my writings that come from my heart. For those who don't know I was in a bad car accident on October 11, 2010. I fell asleep at the wheel. With me were 3 of my close friends. The car flipped 4 times and during that I broke my neck. My friends had minor injuries thank God, but I was in critical condition. I was instantly injured and left paralyzed from the waist down. I died for two minutes but by the grace of God he saved me. Since then I have been doing therapy and believing in God for my complete healing. Also as a result of the accident my fingers became paralyzed so as of now I am unable to write. But I will not allow anything to hold me back. About 16 of these poems I typed on the computer using only my pinky finger knuckle. God is good. So in this book you will read about my love. You will read about my life experiences and things such as how to treat a lady, being a good man, and lessons in wisdom. You will read about my pain, struggles, and an understanding of why I write poetry. I thank you all for your support and prayers. Without God I am nothing and I give him the glory for this book. So everyone enjoy my writings, enjoy my art, and enjoy my poetry from the heart. God bless.

Writings of My Heart
Aunt Brenda

Sometimes I sit and ask God why
but then I come to my senses and just sigh
because the God I serve and know never makes mistakes
even though a loved one soul he did take

but wait….those tears you cry
shouldn't be because she's gone, if it is then just wipe your eyes
if anything they should be tears of joy
while she was alive it was her life we did enjoy

moments we all shared were precious and should be remembered
of course emotions are high when you lose a family member
but to me she was more than that
she was a woman that spoke her mind and always had my back

what an aunt is, she was the definition of
because she believed in God puts her up in heaven above
she gave me so much love and I gladly gave it back
I will truly miss her but I understand her time has come
through the pearly gates where God will say well done

yea was I hurt when I heard the news about her passing
one thing is for sure the memory of her will be everlasting
it may be hard to say goodbye to a friend

but you only say goodbye to someone you'll never see again
but if your life is right you will see her and the Lord our redeemer, just a poem saying I love and miss you Aunt Brenda.

Love Your Nephew,
Bryan Rashon Lewis

Grandma

A true woman of GOD was lost today
meant so much to my family in so many ways
she was wise, uplifting, and full of strength
her love for the lord and other people was her greatest gift
and man her smile....more delicate than any flower a
pretty yet down to earth woman she was with each
passing hour

yet...this hurt I feel I shouldn't be feeling
because she's in a better place and finally got her healing
but why does it still hurt
hurts like that car wreck I went thru maybe even worst
to see her in that hearse will be impossible
but to want her here in pain would be the unthinkable

so the Lewis and Artis and friends know we need to come
closer as family
cause grandma Leatha lived her life to the fullest
understand me
I love u Grandma.

Feeling

Is it friends or something more, either way there is something about you that I adore your pretty smile, your pretty face what I would do to be that man in that empty space, beside you, help guide you give you love beyond measure is what I would do, Never hurt, never give doubts of you being the only woman I care about, thinking about the what ifs forgetting about the right now's because right now, I'm stuck in a lie too many times have I tried to make this thing right to make this thing work between me and her but I see the end coming near no more me and her gave her my best, but she made it the worst, always faithful though, I always put her first, but you, you seem so different you seem to care something so genuine I thank you, for not judging not saying I do now but I held grudges because people hurt me people scarred me but you came along and that changed me, the way I thought, the way I felt, these feelings for you I promise you will never melt never change, what I'm saying is true what I'm feeling for you is for you and only you just something about you, makes me smile makes me wonder what it would be like if you and I made it official, made it us you never once made me think you just wanted me from lust, lusting for flesh, lusting for touch you made me feel like you never considered such the way I thought, the way I felt, these feelings for you I promise you will never melt never change, what I'm saying is true what I'm feeling for you is for you and only you, just something about you, makes me smile makes me wonder what it would be like if you and I made it official, made it us you never once made me think you just wanted me from lust, lusting for flesh, lusting for touch you made me feel like you never considered such vivid thoughts, vivid things I'm almost done but there's more to this feeling I like you, but this is something strange maybe weird but all I know is I don't feel the same about another girl, another one in the back of my mind I think could she be the one the one to make me feel so good and so right I thought about you so much in my dreams at night it's something about you I want to know but I know my boundaries when to say yes or no, but this feeling inside burns like a fire and my feelings for you are getting deeper something like a desire, desire to love, desire to want you a girl who deserves everything she wants, so this poem right here, is for you my dear, hope it brightens your day, and wipes away your tears.

I See Her

Distant, like the sun's ultraviolet rays
from day to day I always say I wish I could see my babe
drifting away, but in the fog I still see her
my vision is kind of blurred but I have ears so I still hear her
I see her, even when I close my eyes
but even with closed eyes the days still pass by

her touch, I'm missing it so much
her soft brown skin makes one lust but I must
see her, my vision is scarred by thoughts
when I look in the mirror her eyes is what my eyes have caught
or captured, I'm caught up in the rapture of flesh

but my spirit fighting my flesh is what the Lord taught me best
yeah her and me we are the best
better than the rest
all the tests and trials the devil threw at us have been laid to rest
R.I.P, safe are we

I mean us, I pray to God for better vision
because where she be, her safety be low, no signs of security
I see her, in her eyes I am her protector

but I'm never there to protect her because she lives in a different sector
her kisses so sweet like nectar
patiently waiting to see her but this vision isn't getting no better

Wait…. Is that her? Do I see her?
oh never mind it's just somebody trying to be her
NO, can't no one ever replace
I might be blind but I can still see her face
cause every time I look in my heart I see her
Wait…. I see her this time it is her.

It's Time Now

It's time now to take our relationship to the next level
my feelings for you are getting deeper and deeper
like its below sea level
I know it's humorous but its true
all I want to do is be with you

your astonishing beauty has got me hypnotized
like Luther Vandross you going in circles and that's no lie
I miss you so much that I'm practically on my hands and knees
hoping for the day that I'll have a chance to be

your lover, your husband, and your number one man
I want to be the man that be number one in your plans
Everybody I think about whether I'll ever meet someone like you again
someone who could come in my life and love me again
I cried when I lost you and I thought my life was done
I thought the evil cupid had come in and broke up what I had won

I mean what I had Lost
I never wanted to pay that cost
I was ready to catch love like that receiver Randy Moss

I care for you, I love you, I'll even give my life for you
I'll do anything that will get me back to You
It's Time Now.

Something About You

I don't know what it is but it's something about you
something that lets me know that I couldn't live without you
Your beauty is pure, breezy like spring winds
there's something about you that lies deep within

Is it your smile, your style, maybe your heart?
It's like my sunny day turns cloudy when we are apart
Baby I'm at the starting line making my way to the finish
letting your love be my fuel so I can be determined to win it
I'm not just talking or chatting all of this is true
I never let myself even think about me without you

How do I put all my love for you into words?
Maybe in similes, metaphors or even verbs
man this is absurd, I've been feeling like this forever
Girl it's something about you
that makes me want to get to know you better

Never knew how this virtue could be so real
no time to chill, I got more words to instill
I mean install, I'm in awe of how I feel
Me without you, that's something past surreal

The way you look at me makes me think that you feel the same,

you had me at hello even though I didn't know your name
I hope you take some time to think this through
because all these feelings I have
is cause there's something about you

Still Someone Special

I see you doing your thing now…and all that is cool you studying and working hard trying stay on top in school still beautiful as always and that will never change but you still someone special so hear me out and let me explain

You know I may not see you everyday….nothing new does that keep me from loving you…what you think you know us being friends…yea I like it is it gone keep me from wanting to be your man…doubt it I still think about you and the times we had wishing I had a chance to relive the good times and go back Am I walking yet…no not yet but am I going to soon…let's just say I'd place that bet So even though you can have any man you want the man that still loves you and was good to you still wants a chance to, be with you but being your friend will never change that's something that will always remain the same you already know I respect your mind, body, and soul your worth to me is more precious than any amount of gold, our friendship is forever and priceless and anytime I bless you with gifts I'm never trying to buy it but as far as us go…I believe we still have unwritten chapters I think we still missing that part in the book that says happily ever after but you know I'm respecting the fact that you're not ready for a relationship because in all honesty I'm not either I mean really not just saying it to say it but right now I'm not but that's why I like this between us because it gives us a chance to start over and make a friendship become ten times stronger as we get closer do I want to be more…of course you already know that do I think you deserve a love like mine…without a doubt and that's a fact but as this goes…I'm just happy being in your life so that means I can still bug you and we can fuss and fight lol, but as long as I'm a reason you smile that's alright with me but your man is still what I want to be so this is just something to address to issue that you always still be someone special so when you're ready to take this further just let me know let GOD lead the way and you follow might sound cheesy but yes I do kind of miss you and in my heart forever you will be someone special.

What This Is

Some call this a gift, but I call this my calling
I fell in love with you but before then I was already falling
deeper in thought, deeper in feeling
used to be in pain but my God gave me my healing
my healing was you, an angel so kind and true
there's not enough love in the world to show how much I love you

I love….you, your smile, your essence
there's no other girl who can surround me with the best presence
So intelligent, faithful and witty
and a real down to earth type of lady you're never saddity
the most beautiful flower, the sweetest drop of honey
all I want in this world is you forget the money

Your beauty, more beautiful than a blossomed rose
wanting to love you forever is definitely a decision I chose
and I will never regret and never forget
the first time we kissed and our eyes met

Looking into your eyes I get lost in your galaxy
and no matter where I'm at where you are where I'd rather be
basically what I'm trying to say is that I'm happily
in this relationship for life so practically

What I mean is that
as a matter of fact
your heart is where my soul want to stay at
and your husband is what I promise to be
and also protect your body, soul, and mind
continuously
I know its early now, but when the time comes
not only God but our parents will say job well done.

What Was Done

Define a goddess
when it comes to her she is always nothing less than modest
my plan is, to make her feel so special
my future endeavors has me wanting to be one with her vessel
causing her stress is the last thing on my mind
so while I'm with her stress free is how I want to spend our time

What she did was, break down that wall
That one just like the Berlin Wall I thought no man could make fall
I stood tall on my own two feet
praying God would send one of his angels to me

So what he did was, answer my prayers
but it took time, just like going up 8 flights of stairs
so step by step and foot by foot
What I did was, put my love in a position where it could be took
I mean taken, because believe me my love she has
like I'm to the point where if I'm more than a minute away from her
my heart starts to spaz

What I did was, make her understand
that I wanted to be more than just her man
I want to be her soul mate, the pilot to her plane

the Adam to her Eve, the Tarzan to her Jane
see when you reflect on what was already been done
then you work on doing better on what there is to become

then what you do next is the real test
you take what you did better and make it the best
better than the rest, better than anything
What I did was, make her my everything
everything that with another man she couldn't be
and letting her eyes visualize things that with another man she couldn't see
and made her hands get a chance to feel
that with another man what she would feel would be so fake not real

What I did was, entertain her inner most deeper thoughts
made her dreams become reality no matter what the cost
what's done is done, and as what's to become unfolds
I continue to give what she needs and loving her with my soul
because with God leading the way our love will never be shattered
and instead of living in the past and thinking about what was done,
the future to me is the only thing that matters

Writings of My Pain, Passion

Abuse, Pain, You

Abuse…these thoughts bring me pain
and with these thoughts in my brain they drive me insane
all I want to do is move ahead
but the little boy inside of me that was killed doesn't seem to be dead
get out of my head, this demon called abuse
he used to use me but as of now I'm of no use

she's back, the one that gave me these scars
all the memories of the bruises are, not distant like the north star
emotional, I cried with each passing hour
but all the screams of terror the walls seemed to devour
beat to the point of no pulse
it felt like my spirit had left this earth

why me? I look in the mirror and ask the questions
and with each beat my heart release I feel the pressure
pressure, something I know much about
as a little kid I had a problem with speaking out
but you see poetry is my ministry
it's the gift that God has given to me

but can he lift this burden
I knew that growing up my life wouldn't be perfect
but why didn't he answer my call
cries for help it seemed like he ignored them all
but why? I never asked for this life
never asked to be pressed down by strife

Wait…. I think I see a turning point in my life
a woman, someone who is destined to be my wife
I see a little clearer now 20/20 vision
maybe these decisions were part of my mission
a mission that leads to the altar
but all of these thoughts seem to want to falter
my plans to make you Mrs. Right
but what don't kill me makes me stronger so I'm ready to fight

but every time I do, I always lose
the abuse, the pain, the little boy just wants to be loose
but you see with you in my life it makes it easier
and of course I give thanks to my maker the great commissioner

now to end things with a bang
without you in my life would be like a lion untamed
so as life goes on and get better
just remember that me and you together forever would make our lives better abuse, pain, you…
despite what has happen in my life
it doesn't compare to the significance of me and you.

His Mistake

Why are you making me pay for his mistakes?
I didn't know that his burden would be this hard to break
I'm different than him you already know that
I want to be the one that brings your love back
because right now I know it's in the air like Bluetooth
and baby every word that what I'm saying is the truth

tell me why I got to hurt
I'm trying to do like that boy Ne-Yo said and make it work
and make it right
I don't want to lose this fight
I'm trying to be the man that gives you a better life
but I can't do that if u keep trying to neglect
when I'm around you it's the best feeling I ever felt
girl, I love everything you do

I love and cherish every moment I get to spend with you
How am I supposed to breathe with no air
girl me without you is something I can't bare
I wouldn't dare say that I don't care
baby you're a diamond in the rough, something that's just so rare

like John Legend said Here We Go Again

baby you're doing it again when you make me pay for the mistakes of that other man
I want to be with you, got to be with you
need to be with you, I start going crazy if I spend more than an hour away from you, you want my t-shirt come get my t-shirt.

Like Beyoncé said you can sleep in my t-shirt
You're more than enough; you're all that I need
but I can't meet your needs if I keep paying for another man's evil deeds.

Tell me what you want from me
cause I ain't going nowhere I ain't got no reason to leave
the only thing that I need is for a chance to be
with you so don't make me pay for the mistakes from him please.

Hurt

Hurt...but in a way so confused
not a thought in my mind told me that I would lose
the one person who had my whole heart
now that we apart, I'm all the way back at start

I was faithful, trustworthy, and loyal
but at the end of the day it was my love you spoiled
since then it's been sleepless nights and early mornings for me
to know all I did for you is now history
Physically what I'm going through is torment
how can you hurt me so bad when you were such an angel heaven sent

this was what I feared most
to be hurt by someone who came so close
to being my lifetime queen
A long awaited dream that was in my near future scene
to leave a man broken who couldn't walk
definitely had my mouth closed...couldn't talk

speechless...better yet felt like a speech impediment
didn't even tell me face to face that you had reached this settlement
I mean a phone call could have been an element
now I'm stuck looking at these walls dumbfounded
like...what did I do to deserve this

once you got used to your freedom you felt the need to end this

but why…all I ever did was love hard
now its as if my heart is torn and left scarred
bruised, beaten, and contorted like you gave my heart a disease
that moment when you said its over surely brought me to my knees
and its like you did it with ease
how can someone who say they love me so much leave me like this, can you tell me that please…

but I'm strong so I'm a use this hurt as motivation
and when I get on my feet I'll come to you with no hesitation
and say thank you for the hurt for it fueled me to endure
who knew all it took was a little hurt to cure

made me look inside myself and find that I'm a great man
and I hope that GOD gets you to understand
that I never did you wrong and I always put you first
but you felt the need to curse me with a broken heart…hurt.

Addicted to My Spouse

Baby tell me what you want me to do to you
girl my body is yours for the taking and I want to cater to you
I want to be your dinner and your dessert
I'll meet your needs and show you what a woman's worth

girl you're my heart, my soul, the air that I breathe
Everything that I want to do to you is extraordinary
anything you want just tell me and I will do it
if it's love making you want, okay baby let's get to it
is that a smile? That's what I love to see you do
you want somebody to fulfill your dreams and desires,
well let me say I'm the one of the few

name it I'll do it, say it I'll make it happen
I'm just a sailor to this ship, baby you're my captain
why am I so addicted
maybe it's the way that you move that got me twisted
side to side, up and down
girl you make my world go round and round

I never thought trying to cope would be so hard
I get that itch every time that we are apart
Day to day, year to year
I'm waiting for that day you reappear… in my heart,
so baby I can start

my new life with you so I can put my car in park
but right now it's in drive, this craving is driving me crazy
this feeling I have for you has my vision kind of hazy
I don't regret what I did to you
I did it because I wanted to
but I never knew that these feelings for you would grow so personal
foot on the gas I put my love for you in overdrive
can't no other person stop me from what I feel inside

you see the reason why I'm telling you what I feel
Is because I told you from the start that I would always keep it real
I'm addicted… because all I see is you every time I look in the mirror
every time that we make love my vision gets a little clearer seeking to find the answer, seeking to find a cure
anytime I'm not with you this crazy infatuation continues to endure
the destination of neutral satisfaction is my goal
even though these endless roads are costly I'm willing to pay the toll

It started with a kiss
never expected this
but I always find myself trying to reminisce about you…
I'm so addicted.

Writings Of My Love

Because Of You

Because of you I smile
because of you is why my life is worthwhile
you see I didn't know what love was
until you came into my heart and showed what love does
love heals hearts, souls, and minds
even in my mind I always find the time

to think about you
dream about you
think about the things I couldn't do without you
I couldn't love, care, share, and protect
anytime your ship wrecks I'll be there to help you back on deck

My love for never lessens like the Dow Jones
no my love is strong like a love Jones
See people say that you break up to make up
but they wouldn't have to make up if they never break up

all I want to make up is the lost time
the time I always lose to spend with my divine
love, angel, better yet my sunshine
yea my sun shines anytime you're in my mind

see sometimes I have thoughts that I'm going to lose you but then I have to get back to reality and realize it was just an illusion because of you I now know what love is but when I put that ring on your finger that'll show you how strong my love is.

Final Destination

I need the proper preparation
to make sure that I reach you my final destination
my dedication and determination
anybody trying to keep me from you is worth
exterminating
steady waiting to make you
my wife baby and I know you
want a man that will take you places

But right now I'm talking about that place which is
my final destination
no I'm not talking about heaven
but being with you is heaven
bliss, satisfaction to a certain degree
can't nobody in the world love you like me

We, love each other more everyday don't you agree
that destination of being your husband is where I
want to be
cheat? Babe that's something I would and will never
do
and there is nothing that I have to hide from you

Rumor control is something we deal with together
by myself no, no, like Fab and Ne-Yo say you make
me better
money, cars, clothes they can have it
loving you is the thing that I'm already making a
habit, the haters trying to keep me from my last stop

might as well quit because our heightened love for each
other won't drop

They say a good woman is hard to come by
well that's why I'm not letting our love fly
as time go by and the destination becomes clear
There's only one thing in this world that I fear
that the haters will keep me from letting my love near
your heart baby, a vital organ that to me is so dear

Staying on my toes as I fight this thing called rumors
a thing that can kill relationships like it was a tumor
Excuse my metaphors but this right here is true
that my final destination on this earth is you
waiting for that day when my dreams will come true

They say there's only a few good men, well baby I'm one
of the few let me love you, that was something I wanted
to do and let our love be the string and God pull us
through because our final destination is heaven girl forget
the haters and rumors, we control the love in our world

So my concentration
is to have the proper preparation
and baby this dedication
is for you my final destination.

I'm Here

Some people ask me why I'm here
I'm here because I want to take away the fear
the fear of letting someone love
the only thing you should fear is the one up above
If I could I would take away all the pain
but I'm only human, all I can say is that it won't be the same

I'm here for you, to give you all you need and more
Baby with you being so far away makes my heart sore
but here I stand, remaining in your presence
where I'm blessed by your beauty and your sweet essence
Never again will you have to be bothered by another man's sin
I love you past my heart, it's from somewhere deep within

I wished upon a star, wondered where you are
you were in my heart the whole time, guess I didn't have to look very far
I'm here for that smile, like a flower blossoming
your beauty is like a field of jasmine in the spring
but your inner beauty, o lord please don't get me started
the intimate conversations we have has me never wanting to be parted
from y-o-u, o I just love that three letter word

I'm here for your curves, verbs, and other things like such that occur
between now and then as long as I'm here,
I promise to never treat you like those other men
Ready for a relationship, baby I'm ready for a commitment
I'm ready for anything that begins with/ you, I'm here for a reason
and me and you together can give that reason a new meaning
I LOVE YOU! And I'm here to stay.

Your friend, your best friend, whatever it is that you want me to be I'm just letting you know that I am here for you.

How I Feel / I Love You More

I'm so in love with you it's like I'm in a different world
a world that only revolves around me and you
you may not realize it now but I would do anything for you
take care of you and let you know that with me everything will be alright
may can't do it now but I could be the one that holds you while you sleep at night

How I feel for you is something no woman can replace
or even fill in that place in my heart that belongs to your embrace
why I love you more than before…
because despite your mistakes the GOD in me made me love you more
sometimes I feel as if my love for you just keeps getting stronger
and I always pray that GOD lets me love you longer

I love you more because you came clean with me
you wanted me to trust you again so the first step is honesty
I appreciate the good in you
and I love the way you hold your head up and keep the lord with you
I love you more just because you are love

the most beautiful form of love on this earth that I adore and love to explore
I always wonder if you feel as strongly about me as I feel about you
sometimes I feel as if I'm trying too hard to express my feelings to you
but I also feel as though if I don't it just gives someone else a chance to
I just hope this poem speaks to you and lets you know how I feel
I'm ready and willing to be more than just your best friend
more than your man
but your everything and more

Even if it takes a while I'm willing to wait…
because I take my promises seriously and there are ones I won't break
but I am human and I believe in letting things take its course
but I can't live in regret or in remorse
so of course I want you to be my future wife to be
and of course be your last man on this earth to love you from now to infinity
so I pray every night that GOD speaks to your heart and soul
and shows you that you are ready to be in a relationship

Till then I wait patiently till your heart and mind give in
so we can be together and do things right
because this time will be the last

we can look forward to our future and move on from
the past you know my legs are a part of me but I'm
still the same without them I can show my love to
you without them but in time they will come back
I'm not gone let anything get in the way or stop us
from living life

I just pray that the lord gives you strength to tough
this out with me and I don't want to be a burden to
you and make you unhappy but by the healing
power of GOD I will walk and stand with you at the
altar and say I do with no hesitation and no problems
I love you beyond measure and your worth more
than lost treasure

In this poem I'm telling you how I feel
letting you know what I'm saying is the real deal
not rushing a thing but making sure we take our time
love and live life to the fullest with no rewind

Just so you know you're the only one I want and that
GOD has already revealed
that me and you together forever is something we
will fulfill
I love you more than before and that's how I feel…
pray you feel the same.

My Ode to You

The most precious gift that God could give to me
was when he made you like an angel and sent you down
from heaven to me
and we…have something so amazingly pure
its something called love that will always endure
and I'm so sure… so positive in my mind
that before the end of time our bodies will be intertwined
and made one… unified in body and spirit
any outside source that tries to tell me different I don't
even want to hear it

Because God didn't make a mistake
he made you to be my wife and to fill that empty space
in my heart, that's where you are
you are so dear to me that my heart grows cold when we
are apart
but from the start of our friendship I knew
that the lord made you for a reason, and there was
something special about you

Through all these years I never did you wrong
if anything my love for you just kept getting strong
this ain't a song, but a poem I write
I'm trying to tell you how you have changed my life
I didn't know someone could love me so hard
and that even in their youth their feelings could be so
broad

I mean you love me through all this distance

and even though my face you don't see every day,
your love stays persistent
and in fact the love you show I've never had, it's
unmatched
your smile has brought me through so much pain
it's lifted so many burdens that gave me much strain
and I know what I'm saying is not in vain but baby
you
are so much a part of my life and even though God
has brought me through

I still pray for you because you make me happy
inside
my light shines so bright because you are so in me
that it shows on the outside
my days go by but each day I know I'm still your
man
and the only man that fits God's plan
for your future husband and king
and no man, devil or situation will ever come
between our good thing

So my angel this ode is to you
you are the sunshine to my rain and the sun to my
moon
you are the water to my flower and the ground in
which my love grows
I love you so much something I reiterate but you
already know
I could go on forever because this gift brings me
many words

but not even the best verbs can describe the love I have for you on this earth
so only time will tell how long we have with each other
but one thing is for sure… my love will never be given to another

And each time I use that word love I discover
that I have so much more love that you have yet to uncover
but as I'm speaking on this poem more of my love is spilling out to you
and this letter, song, or whatever you want to call it is my very special ode to you.

Our Love

The Sounds of waterfalls put my mind at ease
and I couldn't fly without her because she's the wind beneath my wings
I'm flying on this feeling called love baby
those brown eyes I'm missing because I haven't seen them lately
It's crazy, I never thought that through all the pain that I could feel
so much love for someone and this love oh so real

and still, sometimes in the back of my mind I'm kind of scared
but the lord made me strong so I'm ready for anything, I'm so prepared
but I have no reason to be scared because I trust her
and I know that in the future that I want me and her to discover

another, level of love that others have yet to reach
some things she don't know but she willing to learn and I'm willing to teach
our conversations, our laughter, our times together
get better and better with time, so I know that us together will be forever
I promised her that I would never, ever, hurt her or do her wrong
hearing her say I love you is my favorite song

now sometimes the smallest things seem to come between
but then that feeling called love always comes back on the scene
and then I smile because our love is worth keeping
reaching the highest totem our love just keeps on peaking
and from time to time the devil comes in and tries to make me doubt
that another man will come in and put our love out

but I stand firm in my faith and I'm believing that she will never let another man take her away from me
because she is that love that I never had but I always wanted
she's beautiful and she know it, but never feel like she has to flaunt it
it, I'm talking about her body that other guys seem to want it

but I respect her, I'm not with her for lust
I can go without her touch because it's her love I long for very much
because her body is a temple and when marriage comes
I can do my husbandly duties and God will say well done

because I waited, and didn't disrespect our love
that love that God so graciously sent to us from up above
so our love that sacred band we have
will never be tainted or turned from good to bad
so my baby, my angel, my wife to be
know that you are all, is, and always will be everything to me.

Promises

What's a promise?
Something sacred from me to you
Something like a covenant that keeps me tied to you
Baby I promise to stay by your side
I ain't got the best car in the world
but at least it's something to drive

Thinking about you 24/7 you're always on my mind
365 days with you that's how I want to spend my time
I never knew how much my love would thirst
Even though my love you're first
I never knew how much love was worth

Until I found you L-O-V-E
The only one I love is you that's a promise I'm willing to keep Every time I get I get around you my mouth goes numb
I'm paralyzed by your beauty from my toes to the tip of my thumb I promise to treat you like the queen that you are
Baby I'll take you to heaven and write your name in the stars

No I'm not immortal, I'm just as human as you come be with me baby and I'll show you what this human can do you and me, together we should be
I promise anytime you spend with me it'll be satisfactory I mean you'll be satisfied

girl I love you with my soul I'm forgetting all my pride

Girl I'll jump through a ring of fire
just to prove my love for you has blossomed into a full
grown flower It's so sweet not sour and runs out with
each passing hour
Mon cherie amour, pretty little one that I adore Hermosa,
Bonita, I could say so much more

My promise to you is
to give you everything and more
but don't think for one second
that my love can be bought out of a store
Don't get me wrong if you want to stay friends its cool
but I promise there's nothing that I won't do for you.

The Proposal

Ok so today was supposed to be 3 years
and I was supposed to get on 1 knee and propose
well…sometimes things don't work out the way you want them to
but see I'm the kind of man that's persistent
as well as consistent because I don't believe in giving up

Let's see so I've known you for….hmmm all of your life
and when we were together I was planning on making you my wife
but somewhere down the line you felt the need to change all that
matter of fact rearrange all that
but you know what there's an emotion and feeling God created called love

That word to me carries meaning
a meaning so strong feels more than a feeling
what you would call a feeling I call it an engraved piercing
a piercing on my heart that pierced
or better yet a tattoo
meaning something everlasting not intended to be removed

See I got so much love for you

so much that the Lord gets jealous because you have so much of it
well…maybe not that much
Wait…is that a smile I see
you know can't no other man make you smile like me
but what I'm saying is…I love you
and even though you chose to end us
don't mean I was ready to just give up

You know some of the things in this life are not seen or heard but felt
and what I felt from you was fear
maybe even fear of commitment
but you know what I don't fault you for that
because sometimes commitment can be scary
but being the gentleman I am…I gave you your space

Let you go
now it was up to me to either leave you alone…or to keep loving you
and today on the day of our first
I'm not proposing but better yet offering
another chance to start over
fresh…forget all the hurt, mistakes, and past regrets

I'm saying let's become us again
my proposal is basically just asking you to put your trust in me
and to not be afraid
oh I know…you not ready yet…

excuses…because I know deep down you know that I know that we belong together
Muffin bear…my darling… ha-ha
stop with the hesitating and just follow your heart

I loved you enough to let you go…and look where you are
right back in front of me
So what do you say?...
Can we start over again…

I promise you if you give me 100 percent…I'll take over and handle the other 900
you looking like what…yea you see this time we gone give it 1000 percent
because we have no room to slack off
this time we gone make it all the way to the altar

But take it 1 day at a time
no need to rush
so my proposal to you…is not marriage on this day
but can we do things the right way but better
so….will you do me the honor…of being my queen…again…

The Proposal

What I See In You

If anyone asked me what I see in you
I would say the last woman I want and will say I love you to
I've watched you grow
grow into somebody great
baby you are such an amazing woman and lover
the only one I love and put above all others

What I see in you is the definition of blessed
and the sole meaning of a woman on the path of success
sometimes I stop looking at my life and look at you
I look at all the things you've been through
from all the pain and struggle you went through with that other man
to finally opening up your heart to let this man in

I see pride, I see pain, I see victory, and I see strain
I see someone who likes to get the job done
but sometimes afraid to ask for help
but you know what I love that about you, that independence
but baby there ain't nothing wrong with asking
doesn't mean that you can't provide for yourself and go lacking

But know your man got you…anything you need
and I know for a fact that you can do anything you want and succeed
but in your journey you will have some obstacles

you not in this alone so failure is not possible
what I see in you… determination
quick draw and shoot with no hesitation

I see matureness but with much room for improvement
but with the right education can start her own movement
I see potential and a desire to learn
a will to live life and the endurance to earn

I see you even when you think I'm not looking
like the way you have a blank stare when you think
or when you take a pic your favorite pose is to turn your head to the left
see I notice the little things about you because I love you
I love all of you
I see you for you, forget your flaws
everybody ain't made perfect so flaws are common

But I accept you for who you are
regardless of the mistakes you make or haven't made yet
because I fell in love with you and I don't expect perfection
but as long as we love hard and I mean hard, we headed in that direction

I see a young lady who is becoming a grown woman
a fast learning strong God fearing woman

one in a million like Aaliyah, but my motivation like Kelly Rowland
you always in my mind and I never get tired of thinking of you
What I see in you…me
I can look in your eyes and see myself
Why? Because I'm in your heart and soul
waiting for that day at the altar where we will be made whole
but until then this right where I want to be

And here I will continue to stand
pledging with my heart, body, soul, and mind to be your number one man
you are the love of my life and what I see in you
is a soul mate and possibly a woman that will say I do
I see the most beautiful, outgoing, loving, and sexiest young woman on this planet… no girl in the world compares to you

I take pride in saying your my princess my queen
I always make sure I boost your self-esteem
because to me your made to look and be just who you are
a proud shining bright star
in heaven's skies…

I see heaven in you
God made you in his image and an angel you are
you have brought me so much joy through my pain so far
so to end this on another level

if God asked me what I see in you?
I would say honestly say I see you God
I see the God in her

Yeah she is my baby, my future wife but she is your
child and I never want to get in between that
God may have given me you but ultimately you
belong to him
he just placed me here to take care of his daughter
with the most love and protection that I can give you
I will love you until I die or Jesus comes back to take
us home
so what do I see in you?
everything I need to see.

Why I Love You, Its Many Meanings
This Is More Than a Poem...It's a Story to You

The best and most beautiful things in the world can't be seen or even touched they must be felt be felt with the heart
if you love someone tell them,
because hearts are often broken by words left unspoken

When I saw you as a kid, I was afraid to talk to you
when I first talked to you, I was afraid to like you
when I first liked you, I was afraid to love you
now that I love you, I'm afraid to lose you

I couldn't tell you how much I love you
not even if the sky were my paper and the ocean my ink
I love you…it's easy to say but takes a long time to prove
saying I love you isn't half as important as meaning it

Everyone was born for a reason…to love and protect you is mine
I love you without knowing how or when or from where
I love you straightforwardly without complexities or pride
so I love you because I knew no other way than this
where 'I' does not exist, nor you'

So close that your hand on my chest is my hand
so close that your eyes close as I fall asleep
it takes three seconds to say I love you
three hours to explain it and a lifetime to prove it

I want you to know how much I love you
but the words escape me

I love you not only for who you are
but for what you're making of me
I love you very much, because with you I found a
way to love myself again
I love you beyond poetry
See I love you not because of anything you have
but because of something that I feel when I'm near
you

I loved you once, I love you still
I always have, I always will
A man's love can't be satisfied by beauty alone
you're more than beautiful and that's why I love you
the most beautiful view is the one I share with you

Tonight when you look up at the stars try and count
them all...
I miss you that much
whenever you go to the beach try to count every
grain of sand...
I trust you that much
when you go in the water try and count each drop of
water in the ocean...
I need you that much

When your heart beats try and count each and every
beat for a day...
I love you that much

see there's so many reasons why I love you
I can say it and express it in so many ways

See searching for love can be tiring
then again waiting for love can be taking too long
sometimes doing either or can be confusing
backtrack your steps and see was GOD involved
maybe that was the missing capsule that dissolved

Faith is needed then after must manifest
then getting rid of other distractions is what you must do next
seek GOD first not man is the key
because the lord true and mighty has all the answers you see...

But who am I to give advice I'm just a man that speaks...
correction I'm a man of GOD whose saying the words he's given to me
love is patient, and love is kind
in time you will find or be found by the 1 that GOD has in line...for you

You see I feel blessed to be your man
and as your man I understand what you need and more
there is no telling what the future has in store…for us
but I know each day I'm your man I fall more in love with you
because this is more than a poem...It's a story…to you.

Your Love

Steady, smooth sailing we be
the love we have could never be plagiarized you see
Seeing clearer now like I took a couple of drops of Visine
It's like I'm in the hospital but they put my love in my IV

Never wanting to be separated
from her, but even then her love can never be perpetrated
I'm dedicated to her, my one true love
my love for her is more free than any flying dove
an undying love, my desire and passion
Will never be wavered by fame or those camera lights flashing

Other girls please, no one compares to you
I tell these other chicks that I've already found my boo
never once thought about going to find another
why would I when I already found my significant other

Cheating, deceit, something I'll never do
I promise you until the day I die that will never be done to you
As long as I live, as long as I have breath in my body
I'll love you and be your heart and soul more than anybody

You're my air, my comforter, the reason I live
and you know without a shadow of a doubt that I would give

Everything and more to be where you are
In every way and every day, in your sky I'm your star
Beyond the earth there is a place called heaven
tell me why since I been with you it feels like heaven
such a blessing, never stressing, such a treasure,
my pleasure to keep it protected
Never neglected, never compressed it,
your love is precious and never to be tested

Your soul and my soul are intertwined
better than any pie, your love is sweet and divine like the
most exquisite wine so this feeling, this heavenly place
I want to feel forever in your grace
you're my angel, my dream come true
and like Alicia Keys said I ain't got nothing If I ain't got you.

The Love Trilogy

Love Part 1

As the days go by
you can believe that each day I always try
to get myself closer and closer to you
even though what we been through never distracts
me from getting to you

Never once asked for your love
you kind of just did
never once asked for your touch
you kind of just felt
Yeah I know that didn't rhyme
but if you be patient for a little while it gets better
with time

I have so much love for you it's like I have no more to
share
but then I think about you and I always find love to
spare
love to care, so much love in the air
no matter where you go you can't hide from my love
cause it's everywhere

instead of music for love, this is a poem about love
babygirl this love for you is everlasting don't you
agree my love
girl ain't nothing I won't do for you

my love for you is sitting high like its on a pedestal
anybody want to try to take you away from me
they got to get through me to get to you

I fought so hard to get to you babe
but I hope all these scars and bruises aren't in vain
as you probably know my favorite letters are
L-O-V-E and love is exactly what you are to me.

Love Is...Love Part 2

What's Love...? L-O-V-E
let me explain to you what means to me
the L stands for luring lustful ways of the flesh
that sometimes is the best kind of love that you can get
the O stands for the occasionally over joyous sensation
that your lover gets when u say I love you with no hesitation

V stands for the vital signs and the vivacious feeling you have
when all you want is your lover's touch within your grasp
and last but not least that everlasting E
stands for each ebullient feeling that gives your lover ecstasy

see love in a way is very hard to explain
because love is more than just a thought in your brain
too many people have made mistakes because of love
cause they tried to get it for themselves and not asking for help from above
See even I need help cause I know what love is
but too many times have I experienced what love did

love hurt me deep, deeper than I imagined

I didn't know an emotion so special could do so much damage
see not knowing who you're parents are kind of makes life odd
because you don't whose love is real or whose love is a façade
See I thank God that someone special really loves me
because she doesn't know what that does to me

It gives me confidence, a little pep in my step
who knew someone could make me feel like I am the best
like I am important, I'm glad she makes me feel this way
cause each every day I see love in a whole new way
see love should be felt from the soul, not the heart or the mind
cause love should be always true and always so divine

I don't have that much time left before I have to leave my lover
but I always want her to know how much I really love her
cause love is her, my one and only
I love her so much that I would take a bullet for her instead of my homie
Mario said how do I breathe well I can't help him with that
cause baby you are the one that gave me my breath back

I got a new reason to live and that reason is you
I don't know what I would do without you
you give me peace, joy, strength, and all of the above
God finally gave me someone that I could truly love

it don't matter what is as long as I'm loving you
because no matter what life brings I can't stop loving you
I think of you more than a friend
girl you are my heart
and I never want to think about us being apart

so let me finish this poem about what love is
so I can tell my kids about what my love did
Now God's love is the greatest love of them all
he died for you and me and for that I am in awe

Love is me, you, and everything we could be
love is something even the blind people can see
deaf people can hear
love is something that can attract even the total opposites near

If loving is true and loving is real
Tell me why this love I feel is something that's surreal
Thought it was a hit and miss, cupid's arrow
But the love from that arrow seeped thru my bone marrow
got a taste for your love, baby you got my mouth watering
never wasting that love, won't ever catch me loitering

let me let you know how it is
My love for you isn't fake, don't have time to pretend

don't have time to depend, on love that's not pure
Angel I wouldn't say this if I was not sure
If I didn't have the cure, to that illness you had
the one that had all your relationships going bad

yeah it made me sad, to see you hurt
but I promise to God in my life you will be put first
This is my testimony; I just had to take it church
because without God none of this could work

Now back to business, my love for you is endless
I'm setting a new world record; they can put our love in the book of Guinness
never diminished, our love always replenished
I'm here for you till the end because baby this is a commitment
If loving is true and loving is kind
tell me why in my mind I'm being tortured by time

the time that is painful and weary
please tell me why your presence is not near me
but our love is too strong for me to feel pain
our love we have for each other is not out of vain
loving you is easy and baby I adore you and me
but asking you to be my wife is something that I can't wait to put in my memory.

LOVE... The Final Part

Love; we think about it, sing about it
dream about it and lose sleep worrying about
When we don't know we have it, we search for it
when we discover it, we don't know what to do with it
when we have it, we fear losing it
It is the constant source of pleasure and pain
but we don't know which it will be from one moment to the next

It is a short word, easy to spell
difficult to define and impossible to live without it
Love isn't something you find
love is something that finds you
women wish to be loved not because they are pretty or good looking
or well bred, graceful, or intelligent
but because they are themselves
throughout life you will meet one person who is like no other

You could talk to this person for hours and never get bored
you could tell this person things and they will never judge you
this person is your soul mate, your best friend, never let them go
if I could give you one thing in life

I would give you the ability to see yourself through my eyes
Only then would you realize how special you are to me

I can't promise to solve all your problems
but I can promise you won't have to face them alone
you know you're in love when you can't fall asleep
because reality is finally better than your dreams
when you smiled you had my undivided attention
when you laughed you had my urge to laugh with you
when you cried you had my urge to hold you

When you said you loved me, you had my heart forever
for it was not into my ear you whispered
but into my heart
it was not my lips you kissed
but my soul
I can conquer the world with one hand
as long as you're holding the other

Somewhere there's someone who dreams of your smile
and finds in your presence that life is worthwhile
So when you are lonely, remember it's true
somebody somewhere is thinking of you, that somebody is me
love is much like a wild rose, beautiful and calm
but willing to draw blood in its defense
love is a promise, love is a souvenir
once given never forgotten, never let it disappear

As we grow older together, as we continue to change with age
there is one thing that will never change; I will always keep falling in love with you
sitting next to you doing absolutely nothing, means absolutely everything to me
when someone loves you, the way they say your name is different
you just know that your name is safe in their mouth
love is when the other person's happiness is more important than your own

I love you with all my heart, body, and soul
you complete me
you make my life worth living
to have known you and to have loved you has been the most beautiful dream
I can only hope that I never wake up
I've noticed that being with you I smile more often
I anger a less quickly, the sun shines brighter, and life is much sweeter
for being with you takes me to a different place; called love

Love is as much of an object as an obsession
everybody wants it, everybody seeks it, but few ever achieve it
those who do will cherish it, be lost in it
and among all, never, never forget it
Everyone wants to be she sun that lights up your life
but I'd rather be your moon

so I can shine on you during your darkest hour when your sun isn't around

There are a million things in the world I want
but all I need is you
A kiss is just a kiss till you find the one you love
a hug is just a hug till you find the one you're always thinking of
a dream is just a dream till it comes true
Love was just a word till I heard it from you
love doesn't make the world go round
loving you is what makes my world go round

I love you not only for what you are
but for what I am when I am with you
I love you not only for what you have made of yourself
but for what you are making of me
I love you for the part of me that you bring out
We were given 2 hands to hold, 2 legs to walk
2 eyes to see, 2 ears to listen
but why only 1 heart…because the other was given to someone else
for us to find
love me without fear
trust me without questioning
need me without demanding

Want me without restricting
accept me without change
desire me without inhibitions
for a love so free, will never fly away

You're the one reason I wake up in the morning
you're the one reason I find a way to smile
you're the one person that can change everything
around when it is going bad

Your eyes, your smile, your everything, your laugh
your look in your eyes when you talk to me
It's just everything about you that makes me want
you even more
the best love is that kind of love that awakens the
soul and makes us reach for more
that plants a fire in our hearts and brings peace to our
minds
and that's what you've given me
that's what I'd hoped to give you forever

Absence is to love what wind is to fire
it extinguishes the small, it inflames the great
we fell in love, despite our differences
and once we did, something rare and beautiful was
created
for me love like that has only happened once
and that's why every minute we spent together has
been seared in my memory
I'll never forget a single moment of it

Your voice makes me tremble inside
and your smile is an invitation for my imagination to
go wild
to love a person is to learn the song that is in their
heart

and to sing it to them when they have forgotten
my love for you is a journey starting at forever and ending at never
My wish is to be the fountain of love that you drink from
every drop promising eternal passion

True poets don't write their thoughts with a pen
they release the ink that flows from within their heart
Love is a canvas furnished by nature and embroidered by imagination
Love…the irresistible desire to be irresistibly desired
love is the greatest refreshment in life

Love means the body, the soul, the life, the entire being
we feel love as we feel the warmth of our blood
We breathe love as we breathe air…we hold it in ourselves
we hold our thoughts until nothing more exists
Being deeply loved by you gives me strength
while loving you deeply gives me courage
in 3 important numbers…1-4-3…I'm blessed to say I Love You

Writings of My Life, Life Lessons

A Good Man

What's the definition of a good man
A man who strives for perfection?... Not exactly
it's also a man who can make a mistake
but learn from it and not make that same mistake again
a good man can love a woman past her flaws
but take the time to work with that woman on her flaws

A good man...is patient and learns to listen
even if they not in the wrong but the woman is steady tripping
because fellas...yelling at your woman to get your point across is overrated
your opinion doesn't always have to be yelled out for you to state it

A good man takes care of his responsibilities
and doesn't give an excuse of why he can't
now don't get me wrong I know it's hard these days
but men who know God also know he always makes a way
good men are humble, never boasting and bragging
because doing that builds up that ego, something we can go lacking
I mean thinking highly of yourself is good

but you have nothing to brag about if your broke and still in the hood

I mean let's get this understood
man was made in God's image but that doesn't make us God
a contradiction that some of these men don't think is odd
there's only one God, one perfect man, one being
we can all try our hardest but we will never be him

A good man…someone who doesn't take no for an answer
and treats the words can't and quit like a disease such as cancer
a good man thinks before he acts
because sometimes your act could set you up for a trap
a good man make his woman happy, or at least tries his best to
because sometimes women will give up that good man for one that's no good

a good man lets his lady know and feel secure
and gives her the permanent feeling that your love for her will endure
a good man…is a man who practices chivalry and is a gentleman at all times
what happened to the man who opened the car door
and the man who picked up the check instead of looking at the woman with an I'm broke look
see a good man doesn't mind working hard to get where he needs to go

but it's the spoiled freeloading men that expect a handout that make men look bad
I mean what happened to the man who took care of his kids...
I'm not talking about just paying child support which some men don't do
no I'm talking about the man who is there for his kids, help raise them
and gives them more than just gifts but being a father

what happened to the faithful man
you know the one who only loves, wants, and hold one woman
that good man that is trustworthy, honest, and 100% genuine to his lady
and we have these men I like to call punks or little boys because they think women are beneath them
that man who believes in raping and beating women
yeah....those men who can't defend for themselves but not afraid to hit a woman
God didn't put women on earth to be damaged, disrespected, or broken
women are carriers of life...delicate flowers to man they should be treated with care, and not like damaged goods

a good man...makes a woman feel beautiful and loved not ugly and ashamed
a good man will put God first and obey his word allowing God to show him the way and put his pride to the side

last but not least…a good man is all of these things
but a great man…already knows these things and tells others
guess God molded me to be a great man…so what kind of man are you?
a great man who shares with others what a good man is….
or a good man…your choice

You decide….

All I Want In A Woman

All I want is a woman that will accept me for who I am
a good woman that's not afraid to be there for her man
a woman who isn't afraid of being loved back
all I want…is that special someone I can call at 4 in the morning when I need someone to talk to
I want a woman who's confident, not cocky
real classy but not stuck up

a woman who can hold her own without me there and isn't afraid to speak her mind and be real with me
all I want in a woman…real emotion
I want her to be able to show her love to me not just speak it
a woman who means business but not afraid to let me take care of it

all I want is a woman who doesn't mind being catered to
because being the gentleman I am I treat my woman like a queen
see…I'm the type of man that loves to cook and not afraid to get my hands dirty and clean
because the definition of a woman isn't clean, cook, and wait on the man hand and foot
no, no, no…I like to take care of my woman

even though I'm the man in the relationship that doesn't mean that I can't help out

I want a woman who doesn't mind to be held sometimes because a lot of relationships can fail without intimacy and romance
see...it's not about having sex...
as a matter of fact it shouldn't even be called sex
I want a woman who is willing to wait with me till marriage
so on that special night...it will be a night of unbridled passion and fulfillment
and instead of sex...we will be making love

there is a difference
sex is just a night or moment between two people who are lusting over each other
but making love...is when that husband and wife souls meet
not just their bodies, or their love, but their souls
I want that with my woman

I want a woman with imperfections and flaws
why? Because a perfect woman doesn't exist
but I'm strong enough and man enough to work with her on those flaws
but either way I accept her no matter what
they always say behind every great man is a great woman...
the way I see it...beside every great man stands a great woman

I want that woman that knows what she wants and
go get it
a woman who doesn't fold under pressure
but welcomes it with open arms and uses God's
power to overcome it
all I want in a woman…with a little insecurity
yes I want you to trust me but at least let me know
you care and not have a nonchalant attitude
I want a woman who isn't afraid to sacrifice
trust in me and believe that I have everything under
control

A woman who won't take advantage of my kind
heart
I'm the type of man who don't need you to run me a
hot shower or bath
but I wouldn't mind doing it for you
…long day at work or school…then let me cater to
you to relieve your stress

I'm the type of man that will buy you flowers or nice
pair of your favorite designer heels
just because its Tuesday
or take a day off and treat you like a princess just
because I love you
but I want a woman who won't fault me for being the
way I am
but understand that I'm just being a great man and
showing her how much I love her

All I want in a woman…is God

a woman who believes and has faith in God
a woman who will pray with me every night
I want a woman who looks past my wheelchair and sees
and loves me for who I am on the inside a woman who
sees the God in me and that will fight and have faith that I
will walk again

All I want in a woman…is a survival who
won't give up on me or us and that will push, tug, and
pull with me to get back on my feet

I want a woman who will be with me for support when I
meet my birthparents a woman who knows when to
comfort me and when I need to be held because it doesn't
make me less of a man to be held by my woman

I want a strong, beautiful, and intelligent woman a
woman who's more than just her looks…but has the inner
beauty of an angel a woman who doesn't let a little
distance bother her because her love for me is so
strong…so strong and deep that she realizes I'm not far
away because I'm in her heart

All I want in a woman…is real love, love that makes me
feel like no other woman in the world can match your
love for me all I want is…the woman God has for me
because the woman who is for me…will get more than
just a great man…but the man God put in her life

All I want is that one…my heart is open.

Angels Cry

I cry
I cry even when everybody asks me why
why he always crying
because deep inside it feels like I'm dying

I'm sick and tired of trying to please
I can't be free in my mind I'm not at ease
see some of ya'll won't get that line because your reading with your eyes
not heart or your mind it's like my lines are disguised
disguise…Am I an angel in disguise
man I been an angel just open up your eyes

I know we were all surprised when this happened to me
I mean let's be honest some of us think we injury free
I know I thought I would never lose my legs
but I did so ain't no lying its messing with my head

but even angels cry sometimes right
I mean an angel with a broken wing ain't gone fly right
…wrong cause with God anything is possible
I'm an angel with no wings and I'm still flying over obstacles
risk my life cause my family wasn't strapped in
but I got love for him so I'll do it again and again

life comes and goes

you make friends or foes
but you never living life unless you go out and live though
another line you might've miss
living is what I'm doing but to walk is my wish

so yeah angels cry, why..just ask me
I never knew in God's plan this was where I would be
but either way I'm still gone live for him
whether I walk again or not this angel still gone love him
yeah do I miss walking of course wouldn't you
but whatever God want me to do guess what I'm gone do

so love me cause this angel flying in the skies
look at me now and you tell me why angels cry
but dig this I'm alive and well
got too much to live for can't you tell

ready for that day I walk the day I talk again
lost my voice but with my written words it's like I'm talking again
die...not an option God had in his eye
just because I'm alive is the reason this angel cried…love, live, life.

How to Treat A Lady

Ok…let us go ahead and down to business
ladies this is for you but all my fellas please listen
first off ladies are not punching bags
if you that stressed go to the gym and hit the punching bag
oh so you mad…ok that's cool bro
but that still don't give you a reason to hit a woman though

fellas a woman is God's precious gift to earth
there's not a price that can amount to what a woman's worth
big, small, short, tall
every woman deserves respect and love and for a man to give them their all
women are a part of us…disrespecting them you disrespecting yourself
I mean guys really, have you ever took time and just looked at a woman?

I ain't talking about looking with flesh
I'm talking about really looking at the beauty, the meaning of a woman
they are more than just their looks and curves
much more than just the bearer of life
yes women are so much more than what mans' feeble minds think

a woman is an angel

only reason why I didn't say goddess is because there's only one GOD no goddess
but in saying that GOD is both our mother and father so women are still to be treated as equal
yea in marriage a woman may submit to their man
but I've seen plenty of women who do more for themselves than a man can
but how should a lady be treated?
with such precision and grace only felt in a heavenly place

with the compassion and power of a queen
and her whole body should be treated as such not just what's in between
guys you know what I mean
When you see a lady work inside out
too many times we fellas mess up and go straight for the looks

all women are beautiful in their own way
but no we too busy thinking about what our homeboys gone say
we too busy looking at the curves and how thick she is
oh I know how we think
she get it from her momma
yea we love to use that phrase
but think about this…are we dating the lady's mom or the lady herself?

yea see you never thought about that way huh?

stop stereotyping girls based off what their mother look like
they got a man they ain't worried about you
get to know what she likes to do
her hobbies, her likes and dislikes
why when she tired does she always lay on her side instead of her back or stomach
what's her favorite color or her favorite meal

see fellas little things like that means a lot to a lady
it can really get you a long way
but no no…we decide to think with our third eye instead of our mental
and wipe that confused look off your face because you know what your third eye is
get to know the lady on a mental and spiritual level first
the physical will come when its time so don't rush it
and trust me when it does it's well worth waiting for
but if you don't have God, then the spiritual is lost

but how should a lady be treated?
with love
passion beyond measure
better than any piece of treasure
and when the time is right…given everlasting pleasure
or whatever you can give her…everybody ain't the same but anyway…

think of it like this…when you see a young lady or woman
picture a bubble above their heads saying "handle with care"
but then right beside that bubble
there's another that says "if you come at me sideways, I will check you" if you catch my drift fellas

but to the ladies…yea I got to get on ya'll for a line or two
if you got a good man and I mean you know without a doubt he is into you
and really love you for you
don't make him pay for the mistakes of another man
let him in…open up to him
if he doing all he can then he at least deserves the same from you

and for the new relationships…ladies its ok to have your guard up
but little by little at your own pace
give the guy a chance to get to know you
every guy ain't the same
and fellas stop trying to spit game and just talk to the girl

"shawty" and "ay ma" is not any woman's name on this planet
cut it out because that's not game its stupidity
and I'm not speaking like I know everything it's just what's given to me from above
much love…poetry.

I Never Asked / My Last Cry

I never asked to be born
I never asked for my parents to give me up for adoption
I never asked to be named Bryan Rashon Lewis
I never asked to be taken in to a good loving family
I never asked to grow up so quick
I never asked to take care of my mom at age 8 after breast cancer made her sick

I never asked to lose my grandma and grandpa at an early age
I never asked to be that little boy that always shined on stage
I never asked to be picked on because of my condition
I never asked to take pills during class to keep me calm
I never asked to grow up teased and ridiculed because of my smile

I never asked to be treated as a confused boy instead of a regular child
I never asked to be raped mentally and physically by both male and female as a boy
I never asked to be spit on and pushed around like a toy
I never asked to be racially profiled because of the color of my skin

for I shouldn't be judged by my color but the beauty within
I never asked for a teacher who said I would never amount to nothing
I never asked for that one coach that said I would never play ball for a team

I never once asked for fake love
although growing up…that was all some of my friends were made of
I never asked to see a friend I called a brother shot in front of me
I never asked to get a call from a friend turned enemy threatening to kill my family
I never asked to be robbed blindly by so called friends
I never asked to grow up in a world full of so much sin
I never asked to try to commit suicide three times
I never asked to be taken advantage of because of my kind heart
I never asked to fall in love so many times and end up brokenhearted

I never asked to grow up not knowing my true identity
I never asked to have this black hole in my heart because I don't know where I came from
I never asked for the many gifts and talents that were given to me
I never asked for them to be taken away so quickly
I never asked for my dad to have open heart surgery
I never asked to be the man of the house because of it

I never asked to cry so many tears because I loved so hard to women but didn't get the same in return
I never asked to be so afraid to touch or to feel
I never asked to be so closed in and keep my emotions concealed

I never asked to be in love with the one I grew up with
I never asked her to love me for me
I never asked to fall asleep for five seconds
I never asked my two family members and best friend to put on their seat belts
I never asked to run off the road and overcorrect myself
I never asked to flip the car 4 times putting everyone in the car in danger
I never asked to break my neck in trying to keep a friend out of harm's way
I never asked to die for two minutes and come back to life

I never asked to be paralyzed from the waist down
I never asked to be depending on my parents again
I never asked to be stripped of my lover's touch and affection
I never asked to have to deal with this pain and this sickness
I never asked to have a whole in my throat twice
I never asked to go months without food or drink
I never asked to go almost half a year dealing with endless sweating and no voice

I never asked for true friends and family to stick by my side
I never asked for the love of my life to be there with me and faithful to me through it all
I never asked for my mother to devote her time and love to be there for me
I never asked for my dad to sacrifice his time to come see me
I never asked for to be the strongest willed man I am today
and most importantly I never asked for GOD to spare my life

but I thank GOD for every single thing I never asked for
all these things that have happened to me happened for a reason
My life has already been written for me
now I just need to be the main character of my story and let GOD continue to be the author
the Lord is my savior
my healer…my redeemer
I don't blame him for anything that has happened in my life
no longer will I cry because of what happened to me

through me GOD and I have touched so many lives and we're not even close to being done
but I thank GOD, I thank my parents, I thank my family and friends
and I thank the love of my life

I thank all of ya'll for going through this journey with me
and know the best is yet to come
I'm a friend to some and an angel to others
but even though this angel has no wings to fly
all tears from this poem will still reach heaven…for this is MY LAST CRY

God bless everyone and remember that the Lord will give you what your heart desires. And everything happens for a reason. Nothing in this world that is worthwhile is ever easy. Work hard. Love, Live, Life.

Life Lessons in Wisdom

There are people in life you learn to live with
there are people you know you can't live without
and then there are people you know life wouldn't be the same without
too often we underestimate the power of a touch, a smile, a kind word
an honest compliment, or the smallest act of caring
all of which has the potential to turn a life around

the way I see it...I don't want to just be someone you'll always remember
I want to be someone you can't possibly forget
the best thing in life is finding someone who knows all your mistakes and weaknesses
and still thinks you're completely amazing
anyone can give up, it's the easiest thing to do
but to hold it together when everyone else would understand if you fell apart
that's true strength

anything worth the tears is worth fighting for
we all have our own book of life
we're just trying to find someone who can read it and understand it
or better yet...help us finish writing it
and people often say I would die for you...don't say you would die for me
because if you love me enough to give your life for me

you know I love you enough to know my life
wouldn't be worth living

without you there beside me
my greatest fear in life
is not having a big enough impact on someone's life
to always be remembered
sometimes life will kick you around, but sooner or
later, you realize you're not just a survivor
you're a warrior, and you're stronger than anything
life throws your way
never take someone's feelings for granted
because you never know how much courage that
they took to show it to you

never lie to someone who trusts you
never trust someone who lies to you
take pride in your name
your name only symbolizes its meaning
you're a light
don't believe me…just take a look in the mirror
the light of wisdom is driving away the darkness

look at the ground…now you can see your shadow
if you are scared by the shadow that follows you
just remember, wherever shadows fall…light is
always nearby
and you fighting the hardships of life…weapons are
the tangible form of power
anyone who can fuse his or her body and soul with
them

shall possess the greatest power in the land
light means wisdom
light that eradicates the darkness of ignorance and the benightedness of the mind
wisdom helps bring enduring peace to this world
and dancing…dancing is therapy for the body and mind
change your enemies into dancing partners
you must find ways to train yourself

to cleanse and purify your mind
the is the chief…the body is the servant
the consciousness is the controller
the mind comprehends…be aware, then let go
your mind will remain untarnished

have a heart that never hardens
a temper that never tires
and a touch that never hurts
we are all perfectly imperfect
but it's our imperfections that make us individuals
don't be so completely oblivious to the world that you can't see what's standing right in front of you
for all you know, it may be a good thing for once

don't go out there and search, because you won't find it
don't go sit there and wait, because it won't come to you
just live your life and see what will cross your path
sometimes the questions are complicated
and the answers are simple
you may not end up where you thought you were going
but you will always end up where you were meant to be

always remember it's the hardest times in life that
teaches us the most valuable lessons
and forces us to realize what's really important
laughter is timeless…imagination has no age
and dreams are forever
when life's treating you like a rock…become a stone
life is about change, sometimes it's painful
sometimes it's beautiful
but most of the time it's both

pain is inevitable…suffering is optional
always remember that in life…whatever we do
we are never defeated unless we give up
no smile is more beautiful than the one that struggles
through the tears
I realize that in life there's risks
it's acknowledging the past, but looking forward
it's taking a chance that we will make mistakes
but believing that we all deserve to be forgiven

never turn your back on people just because you
found a new way to do things
a detour could always pop up and the people you
turned on may be the road you have to take
expect nothing to avoid disappointment
so everything given to you will come as a pleasant
surprise
if there's someone you really want to protect
you should make that person strong
so that even if you are not around…he or she can
continue living on their own

that's what it really means to protect someone

people make far too many promises that they have no intentions of keeping
keep your promises to yourself until you're really ready to back them up
spend life with who makes you happy
not who you have to impress
smooth seas don't make skillful sailors
fear often comes from those things we want the most

never be too proud of who you are and what position you hold
because after a game of chess the king and pawns are tossed into the same box
anything in life that leaves butterflies in your stomach is worth experiencing
sometimes life is hard
but sometimes we make it harder than it really is
but in life the most important and wise thing is
remember at the end of each day it's between you and GOD…Be Blessed.

Unthinkable I'm Ready

Came in this world, feeling heartless
the path of a sinner was something that had me cautious
being raped and abused to the point I can't feel
thinking I'd be alive today is something I thought was so surreal
meaning I don't know why I'm here
this fog had my vision blurred like a bottle of Everclear

But I'm right here on my own two feet
writing my heart and soul out to this Alicia Keys beat
the unthinkable, is me living
supplying a fear factor to you listeners is what I'm giving
and this is my life that I'm telling you
I'm telling you the thought of me being here was so impossible

But I'm crying...why? cause I'm hurt
I'd never knew life would be so hard on this earth
pain, something I felt on the constant
just trying to keep my head up so I can see my promise
Cause with eyes down, I can't see what's in front of me
which means not even visine can clear this vision for me

But to brighten things up a bit
shout out to the white family that took care of me just a little bit
Two weeks to be exact
man I love y'all for that
I could have been an orphan but I had 2 parents that had my back

I'm ready, to move on and to a better life
better yet I'm ready to see my lord in that other life
I was close to being aborted and distorted
but I thank you birthmother and birthfather for having me so I can feel important

Yea your boy had suicidal thoughts
but taking my own life would be a suicidal cost
clearly now I see those who truly care
thank you so much for having my back and being there

so shout out to all those who give me love
and most importantly shout out to the most high God up above
and know y'all I'm ready to move on from this phase
and my only question for y'all is... who is willing to run with me in this race.

What I Can Do For A Woman

A lot of men talk it but when it comes to backing it up…
well some come up short
As for me I believe and enforce in what I can do for a woman
first a woman will look at and in me and see GOD
I'm made in his image and I'm a GOD fearing man

A man without GOD is what a woman should stay away from
because a man with GOD can do so much more
I can give a woman security
a feeling that not only comforts her…but embraces
I can make a woman feel more than special
GOD created women not only to be loved…but to be treated with respect

I can make her feel blessed
not because I'm a good man but because of the good GOD instilled in me
I can give a woman what she needs first…
then supply what she wants
Some men get confused on giving a lady what she wants not what she needs
showering her with gifts is great…
but what happens when your funds get low…
and you no longer can supply her needs…

I can satisfy a woman's needs and everything she wants will follow
I can show a woman what she's worth
which is everything to me
A woman is priceless, the daughter of a father
and a queen to a king
there should never be a price tag on a woman

Her love is pure, her looks are angelic, and her being is heavenly
I can please a woman past the physical but also entertain her mind
I respect a woman's body because GOD made it
It is a temple, and GOD made it not to be tainted,

But loved and handled with care
I love her who she is not for what she can do for me
I want to be in tune with my woman's spirit as well as her soul
I can be patient with a woman,
understanding things take time and effort
not laziness or quickness

I can love a woman past her pain, mistakes, and weaknesses
because I'm willing to take time and dedication with her
and do it with a smile and an open heart
not a frown and misunderstanding

I can do exceedingly and abundantly above and beyond the call of duty

for a woman
Why…because I have GOD in me
and I will do whatever it takes to make sure that the GOD in her knows…
I mean business

One chance to prove that I can blow your mind
without laying a finger or leaving that tingle in your spine
feeding your soul with words or my spirit you see
letting you feel so sure there ain't another guy like me

Because it's not your body I'm in love with
no no I can fill the void without making your legs split...
well you get the picture
because it's the GOD in you that I would love to venture
because it's your spirit that attracts me your flesh is just a plus
sex well it's not a must but as your husband I will handle that trust

all I want from you is for you to want the GOD in me
and I promise to respect that covenant of yours called Virginty

So what can I do for a woman…?
guess that's for my woman to know
and the world to find out

The Black Woman

The black woman…
define black
the absence of light, enveloped in darkness
the black woman's light within her is enveloped in the
texture of her skin

the black woman…
fierce, strong and bold
outspoken in such a manner that those around her know
who she is

the black woman…
the epitome of a soul sistah
the black woman is a woman of distinction and courage
a woman who is so much more than her color

the black woman is a creation of beauty
a Nubian queen full of grace and appeal
the black woman, though known for her curves and shape
the way she is inside makes her tough and hard to break

the spirit of the black woman has a long history of unfair
treatment
even in today's society they're still not being treated equal
but it's that fire and perseverance of her spirit that keeps
her going
head up high and chest out saying I'm ready for the
challenge

the black woman…gorgeous and angelic
natural but not common, 100% genuine
a little rough around the edges but that's what makes
her strength unmatched
and makes a man mind wonder why he gets so
attached…
to the black woman

with that African descent
a long line of history with many sacred covenants
black, brown, light skinned, caramel
doesn't matter what complexion its what's within
that outer shell
all the same…only thing different is a name

I love the black woman
because she's one of a kind
not just the average but something truly divine
this poem is dedicated to the black woman
who deserves more than just a memory in a black
history moment…
the black woman

A Love Letter To Poetry

My Ode to You

The most precious gift that God could give to me
was when he made you like an angel and sent you down
from heaven to me
and we…have something so amazingly pure
It's something called love that will always endure
and I'm so sure… so positive in my mind
that before the end of time our bodies will be intertwined
and made one… unified in body and spirit
any outside source that tries to tell me different I don't
even want to hear it

Because God didn't make a mistake
he made you to be my wife and to fill that empty space
In my heart, that's where you are
you are so dear to me that my heart grows cold when we
are apart
but from the start of our friendship I knew
that the lord made you for a reason, and there was
something special about you

Through all these years I never did you wrong
if anything my love for you just kept getting strong
This isn't a song, but a poem I write
I'm trying to tell you how you have changed my life
I didn't know someone could love me so hard
and that even in their youth their feelings could be so
broad

I mean you love me through all this distance
and even though my face you don't see every day, your love stays persistent
and in fact the love you show I've never had, it's unmatched
your smile has brought me through so much pain
It's lifted so many burdens that gave me much strain
and I know what I'm saying is not in vain but baby you
are so much a part of my life and even though God has brought me through

I still pray for you because you make me happy inside
my light shines so bright because you are so in me that it shows on the outside
my days go by but each day I know I'm still your man
and the only man that fits God's plan
For your future husband and king
and no man devil or situation will ever come between our good thing

So my angel this ode is to you
you are the sunshine to my rain and the sun to my moon
you are the water to my flower and the ground in which my love grows
I love you so much something I reiterate but you already know

I could go on forever because this gift brings me many words
but not even the best verbs can describe the love I have for you on this earth
so only time will tell how long we have with each other
but one thing is for sure… my love will never be given to another

And each time I use that word love I discover
that I have so much more love that you have yet to uncover
but as I'm speaking on this poem more of my love is spilling out to you
and this letter, song, or whatever you want to call it is my very special ode to you

More Than Poetry More Than Words

I'm just gone speak from the heart
you know I love you and I hate it when we're apart
I've come to the reality that I could lose you because of this
but to be honest it's your love that I would miss
See not only have I given you my heart but my soul
losing you to this chair would put my heart in a black hole

What I feel for you is more than just emotions
a feeling of me breaking your heart…I would never give you that notion
First time I said I love you I admit I was nervous
took a while to open up because my many broken hearts left me cautious
just being with you is enough for me
not because of anything you have or what you do for me, but because of who I am and what I feel when I'm with you

I could never see myself with another
neither would I want to see you with another brother
but I can't speak for you
but I know for myself I wouldn't want to lose you
I mean you say this is hard for you…this is harder for me never thought in a million years this was the place I would be

I never once asked for this to be stripped of all my

talents that brought me so much bliss
I died but the Lord spared my life
Gave me a second chance to turn my wrongs to rights
he gave me a second chance with you
All I ever did was prove that I love you

Ever since age 13… I've been in love with you
I mean so much in love not even 10 million girls could get me out
yea of course there were others but I kept a special place for you in my heart
that place was like a scar on my body that no matter how good it healed it will never fully go away
God has brought us through the worst storms of life
and I thank him everyday for all he has done
but now we are in the ride of our lives

This is almost bigger than us but not bigger than God
I have no worries that I will walk again
I am worried about you
I know being with me during this time isn't easy
and I've realized that you can move on to a man that can walk, touch, and feel

A man who can hold you, see you everyday, and give you what you need physically
but it's not all about the physical
I may not be able to give you what you need physically right now…
but that just means we can enhance and perfect our spiritual and mental

but one thing that other man can't do is love you like me
why…because it takes time to love you like I do
Time some men aren't willing to take
well you know what you got a man that's more than willing to take even more time…
to make you his wife
Serious huh? I know
but that's that serious place I'm more than willing to go
and provide for you that God fearing, love bearing, successful kind of life
and remember when I said it's not all about the physical….
believe me baby you will be glad you patiently waited
when I'm fully recovered and completely healed and ready for action

I won't be like this always and I will be somebody great
no matter what obstacle may come my way I will overcome it
but just the simple fact that I'm not thinking about myself should show you that I care
care that this load or burden may be too much for you to bear
and I don't ever want you to feel sorry for me
all I ask is that you be patient with me

And know that God isn't through with me or you yet

we will make it
I declare it and speak it but if we don't put forth our best
effort…then why should God even try
I know we don't have a clue what the future holds…
but knowing that we are giving our best in this
relationship
gives me confirmation that our future will be just fine

I'm not gone give up because I'm afraid to lose you
I'm not giving up because I'm determined to keep you
a real lover isn't afraid to let go
but a real lover never quits either
this is more than poetry…more than words…

Poems Don't Have To Rhyme
We Will Get Through This

If enduring pain, braving shame
despising one's self for the sake of affection
and accepting misery without question is the
definition of love
then baby I love you
I've fallen in love with you and I'll never let you go

I love you more than anyone; I just had to let you
know
and if you ever wonder why
I don't know what I'll say
but I'll never stop loving you, each and every day
there's no limit to what I wouldn't do for you
just ask, it will be done

No matter the miles, no matter the sacrifice
look into my heart and see what I'm saying
My heart speaks the truth, and it always will
if you're asking if I need you, the answer is forever
if you're asking if I will leave you, the answer is
never
if you're asking what I value, the answer is you

If you asked me how many times you have crossed
my mind
I would say once because you never really left
the road to true love was never easy
I know we've hit all the bumps

but I'm standing strong saying I love you until the end of time
I love you beyond poetry
Te quiero mas que el amor- means I love you more than love
I will walk beside you; I will push you forward from behind and I will run ahead and encourage you forward I am nothing special of this I'm sure
I'm just a common man with common thoughts

There are no monuments dedicated to me and my name may be forgotten
but I've loved you with all my heart and soul
and to me, that has always been enough
I get the best feeling in the world when you say hi or even smile at me
because I know, even if it's just for a second, that I've crossed your mind
Sometimes people put up walls, not to keep others out but to see who cares enough to break them down

Sometimes I wonder if love is worth fighting for
but then I remember your face and I'm ready for war
Somebody asked me why I always fall for your type
I told them she ain't a type she in a class by herself
I'm your poet, no one else's babe
I love writing something about you everyday

I love you spiritually, mentally, physically
intricately, eloquently, positively

God molded you into a beautiful, angelic, divine queen
a queen who deserves nothing less than a handsome, grown and ready to rule king
you are a strong black woman and this I know
over these years all my love has done is grow

You have single handedly took my heart and I never want you to give it back
because I know it's in good hands and that's a fact
Baby all I want to do is make you the happiest woman on earth
I know exactly what a woman is worth
even though I'm in this chair
you keep pouring your love and showing that you care

I'm determined to make this work and make you my wife
I saw your pretty eyes in that accident that almost took my life
died two minutes but not even the devil can keep me from you
when I was looking at the ceiling I prayed to God…and I saw you
We will get through this so just keep being by my side
because our love is on track…so let's enjoy this ride

We Will Get Through This

Why I Write Poetry

In case you wanted to know why I write poetry here's a few words. I write because it sets my mind free. Poetry can make you feel at peace with the world around you. I've been writing poetry since I was 6 years old. I never thought I would develop such a passion for it. I grew up reading poetry from the great poets like Langston Hughes, Maya Angelou, Common, Alice Walker, and Zora Neale Hurston. Their poetry just made me say one day I would love to be named among them. I write because sometimes it's hard to speak your feelings, so I write them out. When I'm inspired by something or someone I like to write about it. To be honest I feel like my life is playing to be just one big poetry book. I've gone through so much and I'm only 20. Never imagined my life would be where it's at right now but I thank God for where he has brought me from. Some of the best love poems have been inspired from the love I feel for who I'm with at that time. The poetry is a form of appreciation. The poetry I write is from the heart and from my soul. I write what I feel. I write poetry simply because…I love it. So there you have it…the writings of a poet, written from the heart. This is why I write poetry. God is everything.

Your Poet,
Bryan R. Lewis

Here is a Photo of Bryan Lewis after His Accident.

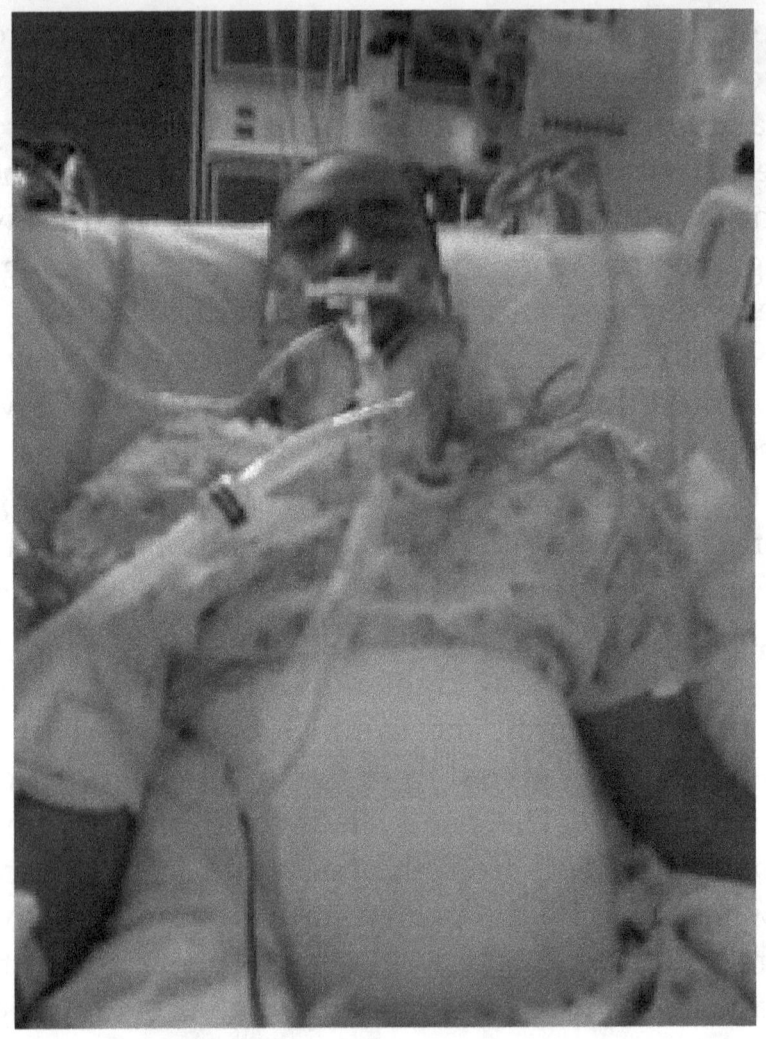

A Miracle of God — Bryan Lewis — God is Good

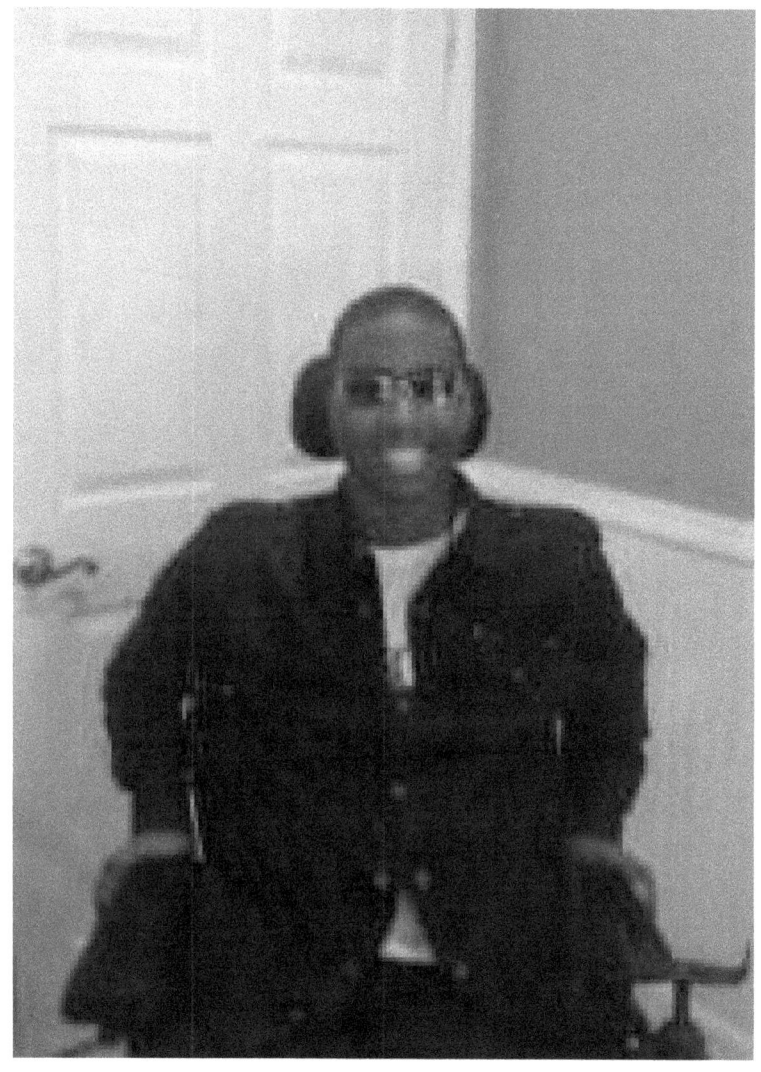

www.ingramcontent.com/pod-product-compliance
Lightning Source LLC
Chambersburg PA
CBHW071714040426
42446CB00011B/2056